BENCHMARK BIOGRAPHIES

Mount Everest and Beyond
SIR EDMUND HILLARY

by Sue Muller Hacking

BENCHMARK BOOKS

MARSHALL CAVENDISH
NEW YORK

*To my father, George W. Muller, who taught me to love the Himalayas
and to my Sherpa friends, who have kept the love alive*

Benchmark Books
Marshall Cavendish Corporation
99 White Plains Road
Tarrytown, New York 10591-9001

© Marshall Cavendish Corporation 1997

Library of Congress Cataloging-in-Publication Data
Hacking, Sue Muller.
Mount Everest and beyond : Sir Edmund Hillary / by Sue Muller Hacking.
p.   cm. — (Benchmark biographies)
Includes bibliographical references and index.
Summary: A biography of the New Zealand beekeeper who teamed up with Tenzing Norgay
to climb the world's highest mountain in 1953.
ISBN 0-7614-0491-0
1. Hillary, Edmund, Sir—Juvenile literature. 2. Mountaineers—New Zealand—Biography—Juvenile literature.
[1. Hillary, Edmund, Sir. 2. Mountaineers.] I. Title. II. Series.
GV199.92.H54H24   1997   796.5'22'092—dc20   [B]   96-18481   CIP   AC

Printed in Hong Kong

Photo research by Sue Muller Hacking

Photo Credits. Front cover: courtesy of Royal Geographical Society, London; back cover: courtesy of UPI/Bettmann
Newsphoto; pages 6, 14, 15, 18, 29 (top and bottom), 32, 40 : © Sue Muller Hacking and Jon Hacking; page 10: © Rex
Hacking; pages 13, 27, 28, 42: © Tom Frost; pages 17, 31: © Sue Muller Hacking; page 20: © George Band/Royal
Geographical Society, London; page 22: © Ed Hillary/Royal Geographical Society, London; pages 24, 33:
UPI/Bettmann Newsphoto; page 38: © Chip Muller; page 41: © Jon Hacking

1   3   5   6   4   2

CONTENTS

INTRODUCTION

In the last hundred years the world has changed considerably. The number of people has multiplied many times and we have seen the development of great technology—automobiles and aeroplanes, computers and flights to the moon. Not all the changes have been good though. Forests have been destroyed and the atmosphere and the oceans polluted. Only now are we learning to protect our once beautiful earth.

I first visited the mighty Himalayas in 1951 and became close friends with the mountain people—the Sherpas. In those days the Solu Khumbu area on the south side of Mount Everest was very beautiful. Great ice-clad peaks thrust up into the heavens and foaming rivers rushed through deep wooded gorges. Perched high on the mountain slopes were the simple villages of the Sherpa people. Their life was a hard one—cold and remote in the winter and cloudy and wet in the summer monsoon months. And yet the Sherpas were amazingly adaptable and cheerful. They grazed their shaggy yaks on the high mountain pastures and grew excellent potatoes on sloping terraces around their homes. They would crouch around their small fires at night and share jokes with deep-bellied laughter.

But even the Himalayas have changed. The peaks still reach towards the sky but the forests have been severely reduced. The Sherpa villages now have electricity and video parlours. You can even call long distance to the outside world on the village telephone.

Have the changes all been worthwhile? Some have, I believe. The children now have schools and some medical facilities. The houses have glass windows and electric lighting at night. The standard of living has undoubtedly improved.

I haven't noticed too many negative changes myself but some visitors do. They may not have experienced the warm welcome that was the norm in every Sherpa home, or the close cultural ties and the amazing community spirit. These things have faded a little as the Sherpas become more like us in the western world. But their laughter is never far away and this almost makes up for the things they have lost. The Himalayas are still a unique and wonderful place and so, too, are the people who live there.

Sir Edmund Hillary

Mount Everest, the tallest mountain in the world (top, center) rises above other mighty Himalayan peaks.
The Sherpas call it Chomolungma, Mother Goddess of the World.
The Himalayas form the border between Tibet, Nepal, Pakistan, India, and Bhutan.

ON THE EDGE

Wind howled off the top of Mount Everest. Ed Hillary huddled in his sleeping bag. He was so cold! The wind stopped. Ed peeked outside the tent. Golden morning light lit the mountain tops below him. Ed's climbing partner, Tenzing Norgay, pointed out the Buddhist monastery miles away. Ed felt good knowing the monks were praying for their safe return.

Tenzing placed a pot of snow on the climbing stove to melt. He added lemon powder and sugar and handed Ed a cup.

Ed dried his boots over the flame. The smell of hot rubber and leather filled the tent.

The two men crawled out into a cold, silent world. Without talking they pulled oxygen masks over their faces. At 27,900 feet (8,500 meters) they needed extra oxygen for strength. They tied a rope between them and started up. The snow slid away beneath their boots. An avalanche could sweep them off the mountain at any time.

"Shall we go on?" asked Ed.

"As you wish," answered Tenzing.

Ed knew if he fell he would die. He pushed away the fear. This was Mount Everest, the highest mountain in the world. No one had ever climbed it before. Maybe, just maybe, he and his Sherpa partner, Tenzing Norgay, would make it to the top.

*   *   *

Edmund Percival Hillary was born on July 20, 1919, in Aukland, New Zealand. When Ed was ten he was a small, thin child. He had never heard of Mount Everest or the Sherpas. He loved to play on the beaches by the Pacific Ocean and read real-life adventure stories.

The Hillarys lived on a small farm. Ed's mother taught her two sons and daughter to love books. She told them stories of her childhood. Their father was strict. He expected the boys to do their chores and, later, to learn his beekeeping business.

Ed and his brother, Rex, worked with the bees every day. In summer the boys checked on the 1,600 hives. With bare hands they opened the hives. The bees buzzed and sometimes stung. Ed's muscles grew strong lifting the sweet smelling honey boxes into the truck.

Even though New Zealand has many snowy mountains, Ed's family never went to see them. When he was sixteen he took a school trip to nearby Mount Ruapehu. He had never played in snow before. He loved it!

Ed worked hard saving money for another trip. One summer day he drove to New Zealand's Southern Alps. He saw a patch of white high above him. He wanted to walk in snow again! He hiked up the rocky slope. When he reached the snow he kicked his boot into it. Joyfully he trudged up and down.

Later, at the hotel, Ed saw two young men.

"They've just climbed Mount Cook," someone whispered.

Ed knew Mount Cook was New Zealand's highest peak. He suddenly felt foolish. All he had done was climb to a little patch of old snow. What would it be like to climb a real mountain?

He hired a guide and headed for a nearby peak. The guide was slow. Ed was impatient. He raced ahead, then stopped on a steep snow field. If he fell he would slide a long way. He let the guide lead him up. Sweating and puffing, they reached the edge of the snow. Ed dashed to the top of the mountain. Like a soaring eagle he was eye-to-eye with snowy peaks and jagged rocks. The green farmlands lay far below like a toy world. It was the happiest day of his life.

After that Ed climbed whenever he could. During World War II Ed joined the Air Force. When he wasn't flying he hiked and read books about the world's highest mountains, the Himalayas. He dreamed of climbing them some day.

After the war Ed met Harry Ayres, a climbing guide on Mount Cook. Ed listened eagerly to the older man's advice.

Ed and Harry set out to climb Mount Cook's South Ridge. No one had ever climbed it. They jammed sleeping bags, stove, pot, dried food, and clothes into their backbacks. They tied a rope between them. They strapped crampons

on their boots to help them climb on ice. That night, camped on a rocky ledge, Ed lay awake. He stared at South Ridge. Could they climb it?

All night the cold crept into Ed's body. He woke up stiff. Soon the work of slamming his ax into the ice warmed him. He climbed until a cliff blocked the war. He jammed his fingers into tiny cracks. He pulled himself up. They were on top! The wind blew so hard they had to climb down. Hours later, safe in a hut, Ed realized he and Harry had climbed what no one else had ever climbed before.

In his twenties and early thirties, Ed Hillary spent all his free time climbing and hiking in the New Zealand Alps. Here he stands proudly beside his first mountaineering tent.

NEW FRIENDS ON THE TRAIL TO EVEREST

Another unclimbed mountain, far from New Zealand, rose like a dream in Ed's mind. That mountain was Everest, the world's highest. It lies in the Himalayas on the border of Nepal and Tibet.

During Ed's 32nd and 33rd years he joined both New Zealand and British expeditions to the Himalayas. He and his friends climbed many peaks. None were as high as Everest, but they were huge compared to mountains in New Zealand.

The men needed to practice before they tried to climb Mount Everest.

Climbing with them were some Sherpas. Sherpas are a group of people who live in the highest villages of Nepal, very near Mount Everest. Ed had heard that they were strong and loyal mountaineers.

On his second trip, Ed, his friend George Lowe, and four Sherpas climbed a dangerous pass between Tibet and Nepal. Before each step Ed probed the new snow for crevasses. With a sudden *whumph!* the snow collapsed. Ed fell into a crevasse. Behind him the Sherpas dug in their ice axes. They wrapped the rope around the axes so Ed wouldn't fall farther. Then they pulled him out.

Avalanches roared and ballooned down the mountain slopes. The men were cold and worried, but they had to go on. There was no safe place to stop.

Finally they reached a level place, far from the avalanches. Ed was exhausted. He started to put up his tent but the Sherpas took over. They gently pushed Ed and George inside, then made hot tea and supper. Ed fell asleep warmed by the courage and generosity of his new Sherpa friends.

The next year, 1953, Ed was invited on another British expedition. This time they were going to try to climb Mount Everest.

The Himalayan foothills are so steep there are no roads, only footpaths. To get to Everest the climbers had to walk for almost three weeks. All their food and supplies had to be carried by men and women called *porters*. The porters wore leather straps around their foreheads. The straps held baskets and boxes on their backs.

Ed watched the 450 porters go by. Some were as young as twelve years old. Like Ed, each one carried fifty or sixty pounds (twenty-three–twenty-seven kilos).

The porters came from many villages and spoke different languages. Some of the porters were Sherpas. The local guide, called *sirdar* was also a Sherpa. He gave directions to the porters. Ed loved the way the Sherpas sang and joked as they walked; he was looking forward to climbing with them again.

The trail to Mount Everest begins in the hot jungles of southern Nepal. It goes up and down like a giant roller coaster. At the low places Ed felt the tropical heat like an iron on his back. Rain drenched him. Mosquitoes bit him. Leeches crawled inside everyone's clothes. They sucked blood until they fell off, leaving the clothing stained with blood.

The expedition crossed rope bridges slung high above rushing rivers. Slowly they left the jungle behind. Soon they walked through forests of fir and rhododendron (they're trees in Nepal). They passed long walls built from carved stones, called *mani walls*. These were

Sherpa porters risk their lives carrying supplies to high camps on the glaciers of Mount Kantega in 1963. Sir Edmund Hillary's teams were the first to climb many peaks near Mount Everest.

Om mani payme hung *(Behold the jewel in the lotus):*
Buddhist prayers are printed on cotton flags or carved on
rocks along the trail to Everest. Sherpas believe the prayers
are sent when the wind blows and when one walks around
a mani wall *or* mani rock *clockwise.*

Buddhist shrines. The Sherpas taught Ed to walk around them clockwise.

On a high pass Ed rested by a pile of mani stones. White prayer flags fluttered on bamboo poles. The Sherpas added small stones to the pile to thank their Buddhist gods for a safe journey. They were in their homeland, called the Khumbu.

Pointing to a dark, triangular peak far away, the Sherpas said, "Chomolungma. Mother Goddess of the Earth." Ed knew the mountain as Everest, the highest place on earth.

*   *   *

Sherpas believe that guests are like gods. In the village of Namche Bazar, at 11,600 feet (about 3,500 meters), the Sherpas invited the climbers into their homes to rest and eat.

The main Sherpa village, Namche Bazar, nestled on a hillside at 11,600 feet (3,500 meters). Hand-built rock walls surround each family's potato fields and line the paths. A Buddist stupa (shrine) stands at the center of the village. Inset: One hundred eighty miles away, in Kathmandu, the eyes of Buddha watch over the city. The Bodhnath stupa is the religious center for all of Nepal's Tibetan Buddhists.

Ed stooped low under the wooden door frame. The air was musty with the smell of yak dung and straw. In a Sherpa house the first floor is the barn. Ed climbed a dark, steep staircase. He pushed open a cloth doorway. Wood smoke burned his eyes, and he smelled boiled potatoes and burning yak butter.

A Sherpa woman dressed in a long wrapped tunic and bright blouse held her palms together in front of her chest. She bowed her head. "Namaste" (na-ma-stay), she said, I greet you.

Ed put his hands together and returned the warm greeting. "Namaste."

The Sherpas led the climbers to a long narrow bench. They served tea flavored with salt and yak butter.

"Shey shey," said the Sherpas, drink up, respected guest.

The Sherpa women laughed and joked by the cooking fire. In the corner an old man in ragged clothes and long, braided hair flicked his wrist, spinning a Buddhist prayer wheel. "Om mani payme hung," he chanted, behold the jewel in the lotus. "Om mani payme hung."

With gestures and a few words the climbers and Sherpas talked about the mountains. The Sherpas had walked over snowy passes into Tibet. They went every summer to trade spices and cloth for salt and yaks. But they never climbed the mountains. Their lives were already full. They had many festivals and celebrations. Every day they had to gather firewood and carry water from the streams. They had to care for their yaks and their potato fields.

Now that expeditions were coming the

A young Sherpa boy follows his father and the family yaks on their way to the summer pastures at 15,000 feet (4,572 meters). They will return in late summer to their village at 12,000 feet (3,650 meters) in time to harvest potatoes.

Sherpas were happy to earn money as mountain porters. Some of them were eager to test their courage on the snowy slopes.

After resting the climbers continued up the trail to Everest. In the meadow by Thyangboche monastery they sorted their supplies. The head lama said he would pray for their safe return.

Just above 13,000 feet (4,000 meters) they passed the last village. No trees grew above there, only low juniper bushes and alpine rhododendrons. Grazing yaks snorted at the strange men. Sherpa boys whistled and herded the huge hairy animals.

While he walked Ed tilted his head back to see the tops of the mountains around him. Spectacular! And what a challenge. For thirty years men had tried to climb Mount Everest, but no one had made it to the top.

A bushy-tailed nak *(female yak) rests beside her young calf. Sherpas make yogurt and cheese from the rich* nak *milk.*

THE CHALLENGE OF EVEREST

Every mountain must be climbed one step at a time. On Everest the first step is the Khumbu Icefall. The Khumbu glacier inches off the high slopes, then drops 2,000 feet (600 meters), pressed between mountain walls.

Ed stared up at the jumble of ice. He was both excited and scared. He had climbed on the icefall two years before, on his first trip to Nepal. He remembered the groaning, cracking sounds the ice made as it crept down the mountain.

This time in order to climb Everest they would have to set up camps above the icefall. Hundreds of Sherpa porters would be carrying tons of supplies up and down the icefall. It was Ed's job to find a safe route.

Ed buckled crampons on his boots. He tied a rope between himself and his Sherpa partners. The climbers slammed their axes into the walls of ice. They used poles and ladders to make bridges across the crevasses.

The glacier groaned. Near them an ice block cracked and tumbled. Day after

High on Mount Everest, Ed Hillary checks the oxygen tank on the back of his partner, Tenzing Norgay Sherpa. Thick, insulated boots protect their feet from the cold. Goggles protect their eyes from the glaring sun.

day Ed and the Sherpas climbed a little higher. They marked the route with ropes and flags. Each night they slept safely at base camp on the rock-covered Khumbu glacier.

Finally Ed and the Sherpas reached the top of the icefall. There, where the glacier smoothed out, Ed set up another camp. The Sherpas carried supplies to Camp II and Camp III above.

Of all the Sherpa climbers Tenzing Norgay was the best. The expedition leader, John Hunt, paired Tenzing Norgay with Ed Hillary. They would be the second team to try for the top. Ed liked Tenzing right away. He was strong and reliable. Like Ed he wanted to climb Everest more than anything in the world.

For weeks the climbers struggled on

the steep slopes. They marked routes and stamped paths in the snow for others to follow. They sweated in the hot afternoon sun. They shivered in their tents during the freezing nights. Finally they had eight camps.

Only a few climbers and Sherpas got to the highest camps. Above 26,000 feet (7,900 meters) the men felt weak and tired. Some got sick with terrible headaches. Even Sherpas, who were used to high altitude, had trouble. There were only two cures for altitude sickness: go back down the mountain or get extra oxygen from a bottle.

Ed and Tenzing waited for news of the first team. Had they made it to the top? No. Their oxygen system had failed. Ed understood their disappointment, but now he and Tenzing had a chance .

Ed and Tenzing made a new camp, higher than the others. All night they ached from the cold. They lived with fear. Would they fall 8,000 feet (2,400 meters)? Would the very thin air kill them?

They didn't talk about fear. They needed all their energy to survive. On May 29, 1953, they woke to calm, clear weather. They pulled on their oxygen masks and started up through soft snow, then over hard ice. Their steps got slower and slower. They couldn't see the top. Would they run short of oxygen and have to turn back?

When they came to a sheer 40-foot (12-meter) cliff, Ed almost gave up. He barely had the strength to walk. How could he climb? Ed wanted to get to the top! He squeezed between the cliff and a

wall of ice. If the ice broke away he would fall 2 miles (about 3 kilometers) straight down.

For half an hour he inched up the crack. Tenzing followed him. Above the cliff they had more ice to climb. It seemed endless. Where was the top? Suddenly Ed realized the ridge ahead went down, not up. They were there, at 29,028 feet (8,848 meters)!

Nothing above, a world below, thought Ed.

Ed looked at Tenzing. The oxygen mask covered Tenzing's face. Icicles hung off his parka hood. But Ed could see Tenzing's eyes. They sparkled with excitement. They shook hands, then Tenzing

Triumph! Tenzing Norgay, wearing his oxygen mask, stands on top of Mount Everest. He holds the flags of Nepal, New Zealand, and Great Britain.

threw his arm around Ed's shoulder. The men thumped each other on the back. They had climbed Mount Everest!

*   *   *

People everywhere heard the news. Some people asked, "Who reached the top first?" Ed and Tenzing didn't answer. They were a team. One could not have reached the top without the other.

After the climb Tenzing Norgay went to Darjeeling, India. He started a climbing school. He and Ed never climbed together again, but they stayed lifelong friends.

Ed returned to New Zealand to marry his sweetheart, a young musician named Louise Mary Rose. Together they traveled to England. The new queen, Elizabeth II, honored Ed by making him a Knight of the British Empire. Ed felt awkward hav-

ing the title "Sir Edmund Hillary." After all he was still Ed Hillary, the beekeeper and climber.

For the next year Ed and Louise traveled to many cities. Ed showed slides and told about his climb on Everest. At last they were happy to return to New Zealand. They made a home and started a family. Ed returned to the beekeeping business with his brother Rex.

Ed was happy at home, but there were still so many places to explore! In 1954 he led his own expedition to Nepal. They tried to climb Mount Makalu, the fifth highest mountain. Some climbers fell and were hurt. Ed got sick. They didn't make it to the top.

The next year Ed left on a different adventure. For sixteen months he took tractors across the frozen wilderness of

Sir Edmund Hillary (left) and other explorers wave from their tractors at a supply station in the Antarctic.
After setting up supply camps for a British explorer Hillary's team turned their tractors south.
They battled crevasses, extreme cold, and blizzards to reach the South Pole.

Antarctica to the South Pole. He missed his young family, but they talked by radio each week. Maybe someday he could take them on an adventure, too.

BUILDING BRIDGES
OF GOODWILL

Ed liked the challenge of Antarctica, but he loved the Himalayas best.

In 1960 he led another expedition to Nepal. He wanted to try to climb Mount Makalu again. He also wanted to search for a hairy creature that howled in the night. The Sherpas called it *yeti*. They were afraid of it.

The expedition didn't find yeti, but Ed loved the weeks he spent with his Sherpa friends. He lived with them in their villages. He could see they had no schools or hospitals, no electricity or running water. Yet they had given him so much. He wished he could do something for them.

Hunched over the campfire near 16,000 feet (4,900 meters), Ed asked a Sherpa, "If there were one thing we could do for your village, what would it be?"

The man answered. "Sahib," he said, (Sir), "we would like our children to go to school! Of all the things you have, learning is the one we most desire for our children."

The two American companies that paid for Ed's yeti expedition agreed to help build a school. Ed hired porters to carry a tin roof and aluminum walls to the village of Khumjung. Two weeks later the school was ready.

Buddhist monks dressed in brown, orange, and yellow robes arrived from Thyangboche monastery. They blew horns and trumpets. They chanted prayers and blessed the two-room building. Ed cut a red ribbon to open the doors. Forty-five Sherpa children entered school for the first time. They sat on the wooden floor, eager to begin their studies.

During the next year Ed received many letters asking for schools. He wanted to help, so he returned to Nepal with a big expedition. They climbed more of the magnificent peaks near Everest. They laid pipes to bring water to Khumjung. They built more schools.

"Namaste, Burra Sahib." (Welcome, Great Sir), said the Khumjung students. The words *Wel Come* flew on banners. The parents placed *katas,* white silk scarves, over Ed's shoulders. They served him homemade beer and hot tea.

Ed looked at the shining eyes of the students. He smiled with pleasure. The villagers laid out a feast of boiled potatoes and curried vegetables.

But in another Sherpa village the people were not happy. A young girl was dying of smallpox. The mother came to Ed Hillary.

"Burra Sahib," she said, "can you help?"

At 13,000 feet above sea level (4,000 meters) Sir Edmund Hillary helps fit a metal roof on the Pangboche School.
This was the second school he built after the Sherpas asked him to help educate their children.
Pangboche is just two days' walk from the base of Mount Everest.

About fifteen miles (twenty-four Kilometers) from Mount Everest lies the Sherpa village of Khumjung. Here, Sherpa children test the new water pipe. Before Sir Edmund Hillary and his team laid the pipe, villagers had to walk an hour or more to fill their water jugs.

School children in the Sherpa village of Khumjung greet Sir Edmund Hillary. To honor him they place white ceremonial scarves (kata) and paper flower leis over his shoulders. The Khumjung school was the first one he built.

Outside the "Hillary school" in the Sherpa village of Khumjung, students dance and sing in honor of Sir Edmund Hillary. Sherpa children speak Sherpa at home, but must learn to read and write in Nepali at school.

Ed knew smallpox could kill thousands of people. He radioed Kathmandu asking for vaccine. Two days later a Red Cross plane dropped the boxes in Khumjung.

The expedition doctors taught the climbers and some Sherpas how to vaccinate. They hiked from village to village, scratching the life-saving vaccine in the arms of everyone they met. They couldn't save the young girl, but they saved more than 7,000 people.

Ed and the two doctors started a medical clinic in a tent in Khumjung. The doctors treated frostbite and many illnesses, but they couldn't cure everyone. The Sherpas needed a real hospital.

By 1964 Ed had built five schools and a strong new bridge high above the roaring waters of the Dudh Kosi River. The river was white with ground-up rocks from the glaciers near Everest. The men hung on wires far out over the water. They strung cables to hold the wooden bridge. Ed hoped the new bridge would not wash away in the spring floods.

Ed was tired of the long hike from Kathmandu to the Khumbu. He couldn't build a road. What about an airstrip? In the village of Lukla at 9,000 feet (about 2,700 meters), Ed found a gently sloping field.

For weeks more than a hundred Sherpas cleared the rocks, then lined up, arm-in-arm. They sang and danced, stomping the dirt in rhythm to their songs. Two days later the first plane roared in. It flew between the hills, a thousand feet (300 meters) above the Dudh Kosi River. It taxied to a stop just

A trekker crosses one of Hillary's suspension bridges over the Dudh Kosi (Milk River). The bridge sways in the wind and bounces with the weight of people and yaks crossing it. Thousands of trekkers visit the Mount Everest region each year.

Two Sherpani (Sherpa women) walk the trail to Mount Everest. Even here, at 9,000 feet (2,700 meters), Sherpa fields are lush with potatoes, barley and buckwheat. Long ago the villagers terraced the hillside and built the rock walls when they cleared the fields for crops.

in front of a high cliff. Kathmandu was only forty-five minutes away!

With the new airstrip built Ed thought about the hospital again. To raise money he and his wife, Louise, told people about the Sherpas. They wrote letters to American and New Zealand companies. They collected thousands of dollars.

In 1966 Ed and his New Zealand friends flew to Lukla. They took over two thousand pounds (1,000 kilos) of supplies for the Khunde hospital. Together with the Sherpas they built it in six weeks. A New Zealand doctor stayed to run it.

After the hospital was built Louise Hillary flew to Nepal with their three children. Peter, Sarah, and Belinda were twelve, ten, and seven. Mingma Tsering, one of Ed's best Sherpa friends and sir-

Sir Edmund and Lady Louise Hillary hold their three children: Peter (seven), Belinda (three), and Sarah (five).

dar on all his expeditions, invited the Hillarys to stay in his home. They sat together by the fire, laughing and telling silly jokes. The Hillary girls jumped rope with the Sherpa children. Friendship didn't need words.

From Mingma's home in Khunde the family hiked four days to Everest Base Camp. They stopped to share Tibetan tea with the head lama at Thyangboche monastery. Peter and his parents climbed to over 18,000 feet (5,545 meters). Ed pointed out the Khumbu Icefall and the wind-blown summit of Everest, more than two miles (three kilometers) above.

Five years later they returned. Peter, Sarah, and Belinda helped Sherpa villagers carry stones to build another school. Ed loved sharing his Himalayan adventures with his family.

NEW CHALLENGES

In 1975 the Hillarys moved to Kathmandu, the capital of Nepal. The Sherpas in Phaphlu had asked for a hospital. Ed flew ahead to start work. All day the men dug the foundation, cut wood, and nailed floorboards into place.

On March 31, Ed was excited. Louise and seventeen-year-old Belinda were coming to join him. Ed fluffed their sleeping bags, then waited by the grassy runway for their plane. It never arrived. Instead, a helicopter landed and a family friend, Elizabeth Hawley, stepped out.

"I'm terribly sorry, Ed, but Louise's plane crashed on take-off."

"Are they alive?"

"I don't think so."

Ed Hillary had never known such sadness. His Sherpa friends wept with him. They placed offerings and bright flowers on the Buddhist altars in their homes. Ed needed to leave Nepal and the terrible memories.

At the airport in Kathmandu, Mingma asked, "Will you ever return?"

Ed didn't know. All he felt was the pain of his broken heart.

But he did return. Three months later he and Mingma and one hundred porters walked back to Phaphlu. Together with the villagers Ed and his brother, Rex, finished the hospital. Ed knew that Louise would have wanted that. When the opening ceremony was over, Ed felt a great hole in his life. What to do next?

Ed returned to New Zealand to try to make a home for Peter and Sarah. For years he hid his sadness with new adventures. He drove jet-powered boats up the wild rivers of New Zealand and 1,500 miles (2,400 kilometers) up the Ganges River in India. At the end of the boat trip Ed and Peter started climbing. Near 18,000 feet (5,500 meters) Ed got sick. His friends dragged him, uncon-scious, down the mountain. At a lower altitude he got better.

In 1986 Ed was invited as a guest, not a climber, on an American expedition. Ed ignored the problems he had with altitude sickness.

The Americans went to Tibet, to the north side of Mount Everest. In base camp Ed had terrible headaches. He hiked down to a lower altitude. Even there he had trouble. Friends walked with him to the road so he could get home. Back in New Zealand it took Ed weeks to recover. Sadly he realized the truth. At age sixty-two his time in the high mountains was over. But life still held challenges. He could tell people about the Sherpas.

He could build more schools and bridges.

CHANGE AND RENEWAL

In 1985 the New Zealand government gave Ed a special job. For four and a half years he served as New Zealand's ambassador to India, Pakistan, and Nepal. He enjoyed living in India, traveling, and meeting people. With him was his new wife, Lady June Hillary.

Ed Hillary and June Mulgrew had been friends for a long time. June's first husband, Peter Mulgrew, died in a plane crash in the Antarctic. Peter and Ed had gone to the South Pole together and climbed in the Himalayas.

June also knew and loved the Sherpas. She traveled with Ed on his trips to raise money for the Sherpas. She spent each spring with him in Nepal.

Over the years Ed and June saw the lives of the Sherpas change. Ed once asked Mingma Tsering what he thought about his mountainous world.

"Some same, some changing. But we helping," answered Mingma.

With medical care more children lived past the age of five. With twenty new schools more children could read and

A Sherpani tends young fir trees in one of Hillary's forest nurseries in Sagarmatha (Everest) National Park.
To help preserve the forests, trekking and climbing expeditions must now cook with gas, not wood fires.

write. Some went on to universities to study forestry, medicine, and business.

Ed's projects brought water and electricity to the villages. With Ed's help the government of Nepal made the Khumbu into a national park.

But change wasn't always easy. Sherpa children were leaving home to study in Kathmandu. Many did not return. Sherpa boys wanted to earn money. They did not want to become Buddhist monks. Ed and his Sherpa friends sometimes worried. Were the Sherpas' lives changing too fast?

The forest, too, was changing. The runway at Lukla brought thousands of climbers and trekkers to the Khumbu. The Sherpas welcomed them and cooked for them. When there was not enough firewood people cut living trees. Slowly the forests disappeared.

Ed started tree nurseries, but rain washed away the new seedlings. Yaks and wild mountain sheep ate them. The seedlings weren't growing.

In the early 1990s Ed brought forestry experts to the Khumbu. They grew fir and rhododendron seedlings until they were stronger. They taught the Sherpas how to plant them.

One day the head lama of Thyangboche Monastery called the village leaders together. He told them to plant trees all around the monastery. In 1995 the hills of the Khumbu were green with new seedlings.

That same year Ed worked on a new kind of project. He helped build a new monastery and a Sherpa cultural center. Ed paid for only part of it. The

Twelve miles (about nineteen kilometers) from Mount Everest is the Buddhist Monastery, Thyangboche. It is the main religious center for the Everest Region Sherpas. The main building burned in the early 1990's but Sir Edmund and the Sherpas raised enough money to rebuild it.

Sherpas paid the rest. They were proud of who they were. They wanted their children to sing the Sherpa songs, dance the Sherpa dances, and know the Sherpa religion. They wanted them to stay Sherpa.

Ed knows his friends face a great challenge. They can choose the wealth of Kathmandu and lands beyond. Or they can choose the culture that is Sherpa. He hopes they keep the best of both.

Sir Edmund Hillary will always be know for climbing Mount Everest. But for himself he wishes to be remembered for his work with the people of Nepal.

Inside another monastery near the Tibetan border Buddhist monks blow twelve-foot (three and one-half meter) copper horns. The Sherpas come from many villages to be blessed by the head lama (priest) and to watch the monks dance at the annual religious festival, Mani Rimdu. Sir Edmund Hillary helped build the balcony where the Sherpas are sitting.

Sherpa children and their teachers gather outside their new school built by Sir Edmund Hillary in the village of Pangboche. It was nicknamed "Schoolhouse in the Clouds" because of its high elevation: about 13,000 feet (4,000 meters).

Glossary

Crampons: Metal prongs that strap to the bottom of climbing boots. The prongs stab the ice at each step so the climbers don't slip.

Crevasse: Cracks that form in the ice of a glacier as it melts and moves. They can be tiny enough to step over or big enough to hold a house. They can be hundreds of feet deep.

Expedition: Group of people who work to achieve the same thing: like climb a mountain or cross the Antarctic. Expeditions often have hundreds of people doing many different jobs.

Glacier: Compact snow and ice built up over thousands of years. With new snow added each year glaciers move slowly down the mountains.

Mani wall: Rocks with Buddhist prayers carved into them.

Namaste: Sherpa and Tibetan word for both "greetings" and "farewell."

Om mani payme hung: Buddhist prayer that means literally, "Behold the jewel in the lotus." It is the most common prayer on mani walls and prayer flags.

Sherpa: Ethnic group of people generally living above 7,000 feet on the southern side of the Himalayas. Sherpas came from Tibet hundreds of years ago. They are Tibetan Buddhists. Their unwritten language is called Sherpa. They have no family names, so many of them use the name Sherpa as their last name. Most are citizens of Nepal.

Sirdar: The boss of a group of porters or Himalayan people working together. Not necessarily a Sherpa.

Yeti: Mythical creature similar to the North American Bigfoot. Scientists believe the yeti skulls and furs owned by the Sherpas are from the Himalayan blue bear.

To Learn More About Sir Edmund Hillary

Fuchs, Sir Vivian, and Hillary, Sir Edmund. *The Crossing of Antarctica.* Boston: Little Brown, 1959

Gaffney, Timothy R. *Edmund Hillary (The World's Great Explorers Series),* Chicago: Children's Press, 1990

Hillary, Louise. *A Yak for Christmas.* New York: Doubleday and Co., 1968

Hillary, Louise. *High Time.* New York: E.P. Dutton and Co., 1974

Hillary, Sir Edmund. *From the Ocean to the Sky.* New York: Viking Press, 1979

Hillary, Sir Edmund. *National Geographic.* June, 1982 "Park at the Top of the World"

Hillary, Sir Edmund. *Nothing Venture, Nothing Win* (his autobiography).New York: Coward, McCann and Geoghegan, Inc, 1975

Hillary, Sir Edmund. *Schoolhouse in the Clouds.* New York: Doubleday and Co., 1964

Hillary, Sir Edmund, and Lowe, George. *East of Everest.* New York: E.P. Dutton, 1956

Hillary, Sir Edmund, and Doig, Desmond. *High in the Thin Cold Air.* New York: Doubleday, 1962

Hunt, Sir John, and Hillary, Sir Edmund. *National Geographic.* July, 1954 "Triumph on Everest"

Hunt, Sir John. *The Ascent of Everest.* Seattle: The Mountaineers, 1993

Moon, Kenneth. *Man of Everest.* London: Lutterworth Press, 1962

Norgay, Tenzing, and Ullman, James Ramsey, *Tiger of the Snows: The Autobiography of Tenzing Norgay.* New York: Dutton, 1955

Sufrin, Mark, *To the Top of the World: Sir Edmund Hillary and the Conquest of Everest.* New York: Platt and Munk, 1966

To help his Sherpa friends Sir Edmund Hillary started an organization called the Himalayan Trust. In the United States it is called the Hillary Foundation.

The Hillary Foundation
c/o Larry Witherbee
267 Exmoor
Glen Ellyn, IL 60137

In Canada: Sir Edmund Hillary Foundation
222 Jarvis Street
Toronto, Ontario
M5B 2B8

Index

Page numbers for illustrations are in boldface

ABOUT THE AUTHOR

Sue Muller Hacking was born in Bryn Mawr, Pennsylvania, to a family of travelers. After receiving a degree in psychology at Stanford University, she and her father hiked in the Himalayas. She returned to Nepal in 1980 with her husband (also an incurable traveler). There, they met Sir Edmund Hillary at a Sherpa festival and again at a ceremony in his honor at the Khumjung school.

Ms. Hacking's photos and stories have appeared in numerous magazines. This is her first book. She lives in Redmond, Washington with her husband and their two children.